6/ 27
signed edition

ON THE BORDER

Annemarie Austin

ANNEMARIE AUSTIN

On the Border

BLOODAXE BOOKS

ISBN: 1 85224 214 0

First published 1993 by
Bloodaxe Books Ltd,
P.O. Box 1SN,
Newcastle upon Tyne NE99 1SN.

Bloodaxe Books Ltd acknowledges
the financial assistance of Northern Arts.

Cover printing by J. Thomson Colour Printers Ltd, Glasgow.

Printed in Great Britain by
Cromwell Press Ltd, Broughton Gifford, Melksham, Wiltshire.

To
George Szirtes

Acknowledgements

Acknowledgements are due to the editors of the following publications in which some of these poems first appeared: *Agenda, Aquarius, Arvon International Competition Anthology 1987, National Poetry Competition Anthology 1988, Owl, Oxford Magazine, Poetry Durham, Poetry Now, Poetry Review, Smiths Knoll, South Coast Poetry Journal* (USA), *The New Welsh Review, The Rialto* and *Verse.*

I would also like to thank the staff of Cambridge Folk Museum for the information about Elizabeth Woodcock on which the poem 'Snowcase – Versions' is based.

Contents

        1. There was a man of double deed
           Sowed his garden full of seed
        2. When the seed began to grow
           'Twas like a garden full of snow
        3. When the snow began to melt
           'Twas like a ship without a belt
        4. When the ship began to sail
           'Twas like a bird without a tail
        5. When the bird began to fly
           'Twas like an eagle in the sky
        6. When the sky began to roar
           'Twas like a lion at the door
        7. When the door began to crack
           'Twas like a stick across my back
        8. When my back began to smart
           'Twas like a penknife in my heart
        9. When my heart began to bleed
           'Twas death and death and death indeed

But

Foxes have holes and can be followed
as torches into their homely dark.
But this gloom that this fox defines
is no one's household now or ever
but Majdanek's ocean of discarded shoes
breathing their darkness continuously upward.

Who can get in to them in any sense
but air feet of babies and old men
who wore them once in other places
before the shuffling off that happened here?
The fox trots on its toes across the dunes
of shoes, the drifts of leather leaves,

just as it did through a field of strutting crows
when I looked from the train for herons.
That was its homely hole in daylight,
it fitted the green as well as a heron would;
and I in the train had my own place there
as eye rearranging components of a world.

But here in the dusk we are strangers,
the fox and shoes as well. The world
extrudes this rough unlighted shed,
it rattles loose outside the accepted pattern
hooped by the planet's curvature. The fox
hurries through and takes its torch away.

So

So I found at the heart of each of his paintings
an opening left for me to enter, his air or ground
or water slipping backwards beneath my walking eyes.
So the pigeon flew in through the Tube train's
open doors and took the journey between two stations.
So the rabbit dug down in the wedge of waste ground
just before the lines of railway tracks converged.

Back to Back

1

The wind in the leaves does not go on all the same;
there is the in-breath, the out-breath, like sleepers'...
The train stopped between stations, I hear
the breathing trees, thick either side of the track
in fullest summer. The sleepers crowd my carriage.
Still as images I see them in their marriage beds –
two by two, back to back, dreaming of other people.
One wakes for a moment, to the moon against
her eyelids, hears the rhythm of his breath and
lapses back into her own. The man beneath her lashes
moves without suspiration, more transparent
than the air playing before the moon. A tree
next to my window turns up all its leaves at once
in a pale-green shudder, a sudden breath. The train goes on.

2

My eyes feed here, this is their grazing ground –
your face, your outline coming from a distance,
one hair on the back of your hand. It is good
pasture, like some water meadow, and I fatten.
This is the way that flesh is grass: I eat and
never use you up, turn at the hedge to start again;
the brain breeds further stock – these languorous
tranced cattle, chewing the cud of you and you and you.

Enough of metaphor gone on too long, delighting
in itself. I like to look at and to think of you,
seeing your profile clear against a wall, watching
you stride the corridor until you're small and
then you're out of sight. And that's the sum of it...
It is enough to fodder me through winter.

3

It's crazy the way I think of you in cycles:
as though your incandescent face
rose like the moon on an appointed day;
like the moon, had its phases marked in pocket diaries;
hung like the moon in my uncurtained window,
needling its light through eyelids into sleep...
or else was absence, its brightness wiped,
as the filled circle on a blackboard to stand for
the fullest moon can be turned to a dark hollow
and then to blank again, while outside,
across a thicker sky, the invisible satellite trundles;
and I think of neither, my diary's shaded rounds
just so much clutter, you in a deeper space,
obscured by I don't know what, I don't know why.

4

Match me, oh match me! Thumb to thumb and
eye to eye, our mirror hands equivalent
to mirror contemplation, dreaming. I sicken
in the solitude. The one glove lost. One found
and stuck up on a railing in the rain. Wool mats,
the fingers curl in to the palm. The uselessness
of that – one glove alone. Throw it away.

Hands close upon each other like the two halves
of a shell. We are no more than shapes of hands.
A pair of gloves. Skin does not contact skin.
Tumbled together in a drawer, we wear the chastity
of clothing, dream ourselves to one...At least
I dream. And crave your mirror dreaming...Match
me in the darkness, bright against the black.

5

Struck wild above the lake by a seven-eighths moon,
the bats make a quick, quick lace in the air
with their flickering passage. The moon brightens.
The lake lies down. Bats weave and weave,
too fast for my following eye that tries to hold
one long enough to see its face of a flittermouse.
A missel thrush hops in the dust; but I note
the original little dinosaur – that throat
of spotted feathers turned easily to scaled skin.
The white moon climbs the sky. I mount a slope
beyond the sleeping lake. A rabbit, startled,
rocks away then sinks and watches, rocks and
sinks and watches me. How white its scut
in the thickening dusk, how bright underneath the moon!

Moon

Kepler, through his lenses, felt a breath
of faint warm on him from the moon;
surely like this one, a puncture of glow
just past the horizon, strip-teasing with wisps
of plumbago cloud.
                I am restless under it,
seeing you exact and tiny in the distance,
working in lumberjack's shirt as the dream
showed.
            Mr Muse, you keep doing this to me:
appearing above a horizon to alter the heat
and illumination here, unsettling
what was quiet and decided just before –
as the moon does, turning gardens from green
to blue-and-white neon like a nightclub.

Delinquent Palaces

I find myself still softly searching
For my Delinquent Palaces –
EMILY DICKINSON

They have wandered from their set places.
There was one at the end of the Lindenstrasse;
the avenue of lime trees showed us the way there
and shook thick drifts of blossom down upon the paving.
Now we find nothing at that perspective's arrow point –
not even rubble to rough up immaculate lawns.

They were meant to have stayed, had been given
exact instructions on the matters of resignation
and keeping still, of offering profiles to the crowds
to demonstrate a harmony, long-standing dignity
in the face of all kinds of seeming impossible odds;
and yet they have slipped away into the night again.

We have to search first in the dives, of course.
A moulded cornice or medallion of stained glass
is enough to be a clue, a pointer down an alleyway
between two unobtrusive tenement buildings
to where a dim lamp winks in the semi-dark
and doors and windows close in sudden chorus.

Softly, softly we go around unknown corners
to catch them out, to find them *in flagrante*,
posturing against dilapidated walls and gable ends,
if we can; we have looked a long time already,
finding only spots where their carvings scarred the plaster,
where their pinnacles were glimpsed once in the dawn.

Getting Away

Houdini in the knots, the rope going
one hundred times around, in a hemp tube
or sack strait-jacket – easy, a doddle;
even the chains slip loosely, loudly down
to make a ring around your shoes...

If I were with you, I am not sure
I could do it: I would crack at the lungs
in the tank of water, my hands still tied,
or lose the race with the fire at the cable's end,
letting you down in the act in front of an audience.

I am half in love with knots, their twining intricacy,
the twist and twist again of thigh-thick ships' ropes
where they lie across wharves, the immense chains
in swathes and drifts on the side of the dock.
It is difficult to leave, to cast loose the moorings

however rusty, however the cranes
have been dismantled and the cuts and backs
left mainly to swans and drifting garbage...
Anyway, I have no part in your escaping drama
unless as a handkerchief-waver growing smaller,

unless as a spectator on the edge of the wondering crowd
as you step from your bonds with a casual salutation,
step into some limousine that waits for you
with its engine quietly running, and run away
from the rest of us struck immobile by your going.

The New World

To begin again –
going in either direction,
but ever between east and west,
proclaiming some relation to the sun
that is infinitely old yet new and new again...

Those girls from Trinidad,
with suitcases lined with khus khus
and gold rings in their ears,
flew east to an English convent school
as much in search of the new
as Ralegh going to Guiana:
his Eden – infinitely old and yet
a virgin land, unriven by the plough.

The sun drags – or repels.
Pale from a string of English winters
then wracked with prison agues,
that tall knight yearned after sun,
went with it, ever towards the west,
keeping it in his sight as long as might be.

Those girls were white with a tropical enervation
from lives spent on shaded verandahs,
driven in by noon, and the shutters closed.
Their first English snows were a wonder –
some million camellia petals shed;
and for Ralegh there were oysters
that clung to the strange mangrove branches,
then Trinidad's lake of black pitch.

To Ralegh in the Tower

Your prison bulks against the sky in the remembered way;
but framing its black is an orange-grey darkness
that distracts from the navigators' lights –
a girl born in Golders Green, in good faith told me,
'There are no stars over London.'...Sometimes
the moon breaks through like a white-knuckled fist
or a pale fingernail that scratches at the eyes.

How rarely any kind of moon coincides with
your small window. A candle has to do
for that bright ship bearing its Cynthia or Diana
through the sky.
                How the moon extends the night,
spreading it like a table with extraordinary linen!
How a candle gathers a room in rings towards it,
holds the walls tight against its flame!
                              You spread
your page in this restricted circle, asking the world
to settle there. You read the stars in the gap
in your prison wall, building broad constellations,
maps of heaven, out of their wheeling fragments.

I try to recreate you whole. Against the odds.
Here ravens take the fresh meat they are given
and bury it to putrefy, ripe for eating.
They are sleek, strutting close to our shoes
with knowing eyes. They monitor disintegration.
Blood spills. A head lies at its owner's warm feet.
Your embalmed skull is kept from your body's grave.

Just so the body's prison holds you
inside these wraps of stone, away from real vision
of green Guianan forests where the deer come down
to drink, or of the ocean in the sunshine
all-over silver-slashed with flying fish.

I think of Lake Como, where fishes in the shallows
swim as dense and ordered as rain falling lying down.

Drawings of Water

1

A country stated, on the page, laid flat
(flat above all things) and exactly limned
as for a Book of Hours: colours ground down
from jewels – shining, little, in my hands.

Palms draw apart to mark the borders,
book ends – the two towers (or, one a bundle,
bunch of towers, the other lopped and broken).
Right or left irrelevant: cathedral, abbey ruin,

land and the sky between. Big sky, low land
and little, criss-crossed with water lines;
stiff trees like sprouting pencils sticking up
into a dome's interior of cloud – or wind, leaning,

leaning against the towers, trees and black ticks
of birds. Land shines with water, scrawls
an idle moving light across white ceilings
of occasional brick houses jewelled with wet.

2

I remember a marvellous dream of that country's
annual flood, when ditches and rivers, rising,
overlaid the land with a thin water skin
no deeper (in this dream) than any shoe sole;

and I looked down upon it from much higher
than a bird, seeing flat shining water slip under
ruffled sea – as simply as one piece of paper
slides underneath another. I should like to draw

on such a page, where the borders of light and wet
are overlapping. In the abbey's open ruins, holes brim
in the lace, absence is more substantial than the stone;
in the moat below the cathedral, reflections

of brilliant swans waver, are sunlight tunnelling
through dark (the building up above them bleaches out);
in a brick house in winter, islanded by flood,
wave after wave of light breaks on the ceiling.

The Dresses

They contain someone; as a painted china jug
contains the orange juice or milk, the dresses
stand, and she within them is more liquid
than the pink, the white, the blue – hanging
from left to right along one shortish wall
inside Vienna's Kunsthistorisches Museum.

I know her name. I read it on the labels
that mention once again the white, the blue,
the pink: 'The Infanta Margarita Teresa in...'
and then the jug identified, its colour fixed
against the potential centuries of fading;
meanwhile the royal child recedes...

In several senses: you have to look her up
to find her provenance among the Spanish
Hapsburgs, the marriage to an Austrian uncle
that brought her portraits here; and still
she is not known in any real way, though
blue and pink and white can claim lifelong acquaintance.

Besides, track her from left to right
and watch her self withdraw, the head
and hands each time less of the picture,
smaller proportion of the whole in which
the pink and white and blue balloon,
reach to the gilded frame, invade the corners.

And on her face a lessening assertion:
she who, at two or three, in pink,
stared back towards Velázquez somewhat crossly,
by five, in white, is dutifully a model;
and – in inflated blue, trapunto-trimmed,
encumbered by a dark fur tube of muff

depending from her fingers and longer than her arm,
while from her other hand some rosettes hang –
at eight has come to be possessed by doubt.
She has her dignity, but confidence is gone,
her glance would sidle past us if it could;
what she can look out on has made her anxious.

I want to say, this girl-child has the blues;
teal hue of the embellished swollen jug
tints the thin milk within, until
this last dress of the series usurps
her eyes and skin, goes on beyond
its wristbands and lace collar – wins.

Green Belt

The motorway has split
the enchanted wood in two,
and fairishes back away
behind the old encrusted oaks
that were once at a forest's centre.

Queen Morgan and her ladies
dragging damp green velvets
camp and move and camp again,
but the wind and rain
still bring the noise of lorries to them

to intercept their spells.
The castle cannot quite materialise
or the great thorn hedge rise
across the prince's path –
if there were stopping on the highway

for such a hitch-hiker
to climb down in long-toed shoes
from the juggernaut's step
at just this greenwood.
The owl looks on morosely,

the falcon that was once a maiden
trails her tattered jesses
through stag-headed trees.
The acid rain falls slow.
A car is stalled over on the hard shoulder.

Consumption

A window filled with roots,
the ivy that drank the port-cask dry
through its oozing cork, flowers using up
the air of the sick in the night ward...

'You are what you eat'; and an Eskimo shaman
said, 'Life's greatest danger lies in the fact
that men's food consists entirely of souls'.
The child tastes coal and clay, gnaws indiarubbers,
chews earthworms. The quicksands swallow horses
with their loads, the long string of them all together.

Keats and the Brontës and Marguerite Gautier were
nibbled thin at the teeth of their tuberculosis
called consumption; this is the same –
the mechanical-digger's saw-mouth at the sheer edge
of the quarry, or bulldozer bashing down
the suddenly-delicate forest's thick treetrunks...

Just what is not a soul in such great feeding?
The flowers and the ivy drink men's nourishment,
the quicksand sips their bones. Eat and be eaten
is the way of it: each of us in the lips of something
with our own mouths full – then gorging on trees
and fallow ground for a coffin and somewhere to lie down.

Caption

*A group of children learning to make scarecrows
at a working farm museum in Witney, Oxfordshire,
are taking their lunch break.*

INDEPENDENT ON SUNDAY
13 May 1990

It is an after-battlefield with seven corpses
dressed and half-dressed in a kind of uniform –
there were, after all, the Confederate forces
who fought in the end both in butternut and grey,
and this is a monochrome newspaper protrait

of construction resembling a calculated carnage
on the clean straw of the yard. It is quiet now,
they are framed in spaces; the other army
has marched away through a field of scarecrows
in riddled greatcoats with buttons tarnished

or fallen to the ground under the greying stubble
and poppy-petal blood. The day is too dull
to give these bodies shadow; the dark huddles
into their backs and knees, and arms outstretched
where they await their crosses, the hoisting upward

against a mottled sky – crows fly from their shoulders
like blown rags. I read of the Vietnam dead
buried shallow in a river beach, and as the soldiers
watched, some unexpected rigor tugged those hands
and arms up through the sand to signal boldly

as this cadaver does now in the photo's foreground –
the only one to gesture. There is an urgency
about his lifted elbow, the admonishing forefinger;
it makes me see the scene, when the mentioned children
began their lunchbreak and enemy executioners forged in.

Innards

After the bomb
that levelled the house with the pavement
so that no brick lay straight upon another:
slightly retarded, the mattresses', pillows'
feathers fell, to crust the rubble whitely.

It was an absolute gutting, the innermost
innards of the house exposed and
laid on the ground in the open air.

Our house was entrailed with horsehair,
four inches deep beneath the upstairs floorboards.
It leaked into the rugs and scratched
our naked feet in the dark of the night.

They found an arm clutching a ten-shilling note
under the ruin of the feather house. Upstairs,
we walked over so many, many horses.

Snowcase – Versions

1. *Saturday 2nd February 1799*

'It was a black night – and a white night too,
of course. The black was thick dark
without stars, and made of whiteness
whirling up against the lips, the nostrils.
Stupid to be out in it,
but three parts on the way already
when it thickened up real bad,
black with the furious whiteness.

And the wind in the ears like horses,
so you couldn't hear the real horse
underneath it, plodding, dragging its hooves.'

'I'd doubt that Bet Woodcock heard anything
beyond the buzzing in her ears of her own blood
hot with ale and all the tavern fires
she'd so far sat down by on the way.'

'Hush now! Be charitable.
Look what she went through after:
those little black pads of fingerless hands,
the feet unmentionable under the bedclothes.'

'And all the drink she wanted.'

'Held to her mouth by someone else
or clamped in the fierce vise of her wristbones.'

'And a land already flat flattened out still further,
the ditches filling, the humps that had been islands
levelling down, trees shrunk to bushes
– all out of sight in the flying dark,
the horse's feet gradually losing
their usual knowledge on the softening, lifting road.'

'Was that when the meteor came,
with a great burst of white light
to unveil the whitened landscape,

and the horse in its fear reared up
and threw Eliza Woodcock in the snow?'

'I haven't heard that story.'

'Oh yes. There was a fizzing and a whizzing
past their shoulders, and it struck the ground
not far away, so the earth shook and
the horse shook and reared up frightened,
and she fell into the snow, down and down.'

'I know about her falling, and the horse gone
into darkness, so that she was alone
with snow coming over her shoes
somewhere she didn't recognise.'

'Probably couldn't see straight by that time,
anyway. Relied on the animal to know the way
for both of them. Never seen the road sober.
Didn't see it sober now.
She could have been in another country.'

'She was in another country,
a country that was a white sea,
or else an endless field of rumpled bedclothes
with the sleepers gone. And over all
the wildly-chequered, moving-spotted night.
You might have lost yourself too.'

'Maybe. But I know what I wouldn't have done –
that's sat down under a bush in a blizzard,
then peacefully dropped off to sleep in the storm.
That was asking for trouble. I'd have known it.'

'I thought the horse had thrown her into a ditch.'

'There's sixpenny and there's shilling versions
of this story. The meteor, for example –
that must have come expensive.'

'It's frankly my opinion she didn't get caught
in the drift that night. No one else ever lasted
as long as Lizzie's supposed to have done.
I think she was drunk somewhere some time,
and the snow closed in upon her

a day or so later than they say.
Though she spent enough hours and hours
in her white closet – that I'll admit.'

2. *Saturday 2nd February to Sunday 10th February 1799*

'You think of underground as blackness,
but what is the colour of an underground of snow,
how white is it seven feet down?

Whether Elizabeth fell into a ditch
or rested under a bush that was drifted over,
she was that deep when they found her,
after eight nights and eight days of it.'

'I imagine a pale-lit cave
in early-morning shades of bluish, greyish,
its walls faintly shining from the slow
melt-and-freeze of her breathing.'

'She said that she pushed at the snow
to make some room. The palms of her hands
would have tamped and polished it.'

'As long as those hands could function,
before they froze to useless paddles.'

'There must have been some light,
since she kept account of the passing days;
the grey must have dipped then brightened,
or a species of black seeped into her cellar nightly.'

'She said she could hear people passing on the road –
maybe that's how she knew it was daytime.
Though she wouldn't have known what road
she was on, or the habits of the people
in that supposed district, or just how the snowfall
had changed them; the chances of conversation
in the small hours of the night were surely
remote enough, and she'd have seen that.

Picture her yelling and yelling
to all those passing voices, and the snowdrift
as good as a gag against her mouth.'

28

'But if she could hear them,
why couldn't they hear her?'

'Maybe they did and dismissed it.

If you were talking to someone as you walked
and thought you heard a cry from a smooth bank
of white unmarked by even the feet of birds,
wouldn't you decide it was a kind of illusion,
a strange trick of distance in that new snowplace,
or else believe the ground was somehow haunted
and hasten your steps to get past it?

Who would, after all, admit to have heard her call,
once they had dug her out from the eight-day storage?'

'She was pickled – at least partly –
and that's what kept her alive so long.
She had the heat of that journey's drinking in her.
She was good as a full barrel set upright in the snow.'

'What kept her alive was the nuts in her pocket,
and the lucky little silver nutcracker she had.'

'And for how many days of the eight
could those slowly freezing fingers
close about such as a silver nutcracker
or manage to pick apart
the crushed-together shells and kernels?

I think she ate and drank the snow
without her useless hands.

She sat, inexorably set into her sitting,
the body's heat draining inward to its core,
the extremities abandoned, so her feet first
grew numb then ceased to be there as far as feeling,
then her hands, her legs, her arms...
Only a little warmth to keep heart and head
alive. Her mouth moved in slow motion,
licking the snow-chamber walls.'

3. *Sunday 10th February 1799*

'William Muney – or William Muncey –
in the warm ditch of his feather-bed,
woke suddenly in the dark that morning,
having dreamed of a white winter hare
that ran into a hole and disappeared.

It stood for Bess Woodcock, he was sure,
that she too was gone into a hole somewhere;
so he rose and donned his clothes
and set out with a stick to find her.'

'William Muncey – or Muney –
had a dream of a great, white, red-eyed, drunken hare,
so he knew who it was at once
and carefully watched its antics
as it zigzagged uncertainly over a field of snow
then dug a hole in a bank for sleeping-off shelter.

So he rose and reluctantly struggled into his clothes
and set out with a stick to find that covert.'

'William, later the church clerk of Impington,
was walking to Sunday service
over the billowed and tumbled snowy fields,
a knobbed walking-stick in his hand as usual.

It was calm and sun-bright by that time.
The dazzle of white sharpened everything he saw –
the edges, colours, each twig of the frozen trees;
then the splash of red handkerchief on the snow
that made him think of the missing Mrs Woodcock.

He began to probe with his stick and dig about.'

'Wait a minute! Wait a minute!
Why should such a find cause him to look for her?

Didn't this Elizabeth edge squares of white linen
with lace she had made herself, like other women?
Didn't she, like them, leave red kerchiefs to the men?'

'Maybe it was really some scarlet female clothing
like flannel drawers or a petticoat. Perhaps William
made it mentionable for listeners later on.'

'And how did such a garment happen to be lying
on top of the snow in that casual fashion?'

'I heard Eliza tied whatever the red thing was
to the end of a branch, poked it up through the drift.'

'Which would need a convenient seven-foot pole,
considerable strength and functioning, even dextrous, fingers!

Then envisage the removal of that petticoat
or drawers from legs that had long gone dead
under several thick skirts and the folds of a mantle,
with again the problematical-because-frozen hands.'

'It was the purest accident.

Sounding ahead with his stick, like any wise walker
in such a snowed-under, featureless landscape,
he felt the ashplant sink too deep;
and at last someone heard a cry –
though now it was much fainter than before –
from what for eight days had been
a lump or a bank or a flat place of hollow snow.'

'Just because your account is the last of a list,
don't think it will be the definitive version.
It won't, you know. It's only another story.'

'And so they dug her out and carried her –
making a chair of their hands,
since they feared to unlock her yet
from that sitting posture – to her home
and her circling children, to warm broth
between the lips, and a six-months career
as some sort of wonder of the world.'

4. Sunday 10th February to Wednesday 24th July 1799

'Why did so many come to hear her story?'

'Why are we here now, trying to thrash it out?'

'But to pay up to a day's wages
to sit beside her ripe-smelling rumpled bed
with the ale jug next to it, to watch those hands
that were like the naked blackened paws
of an unknown animal; just to hear
from her own lips the variable stories –
memory laced with drink and imagination,
or fancy lightly pricked with recollection.'

'From her own lips. To say "I was there
and personally heard her memories."
To say "I felt the weight and stiffness
of those hands, I helped her to a drink,
and she told me what she had never revealed
before." Here something like the meteor would come in.'

'Needing the mystery and wonder.
Needing to believe life is stronger than death
after all; that an ordinary woman
buried longer than Christ, could rise
and live on to lie in relative comfort,
attended by her children, drinking as much as she liked.'

'I don't believe it was Lizzie who changed the versions.
You know how these legends grow,
passed as it were from hand to hand,
embroidery added where there's plainness,
the listener's own explanations put in
where the cause of an effect seems lacking.

Suppose Elizabeth Woodcock wanted to bear witness,
tell the details of her fate as clearly as she could;
do you think anyone would have let her leave it
unvarnished, plus the dark gaps come from sleeping
or the failure of memory? They must add
their decoration every time. We are embellishing now.'

'She woke often in the night
to beat back the bedclothes
rising towards her chin
like an awful snowdrift.'

'With her stomach a sudden cave of hunger
that must be filled by something, anything.'

'She grew glad to see her nightgowns
grey with wearing, newly abhorring whiteness.'

'And the clinical cold smell of snow
could only be wiped out with richness –
apples rotting into ferment, sweat stiff in the sheets,
the baby's yellow faeces inexpertly cleaned away.'

'The drink was a delicious heat
washing away her memory of cold,
of time, the white and black together.
Drink was a delightful blurring:
every colour into mixture,
every minute joining others
till thought of the snowcave snowcase
brought with it befores and afters –
no nightmare, part of history, just life.'

'So the drink was what she died of in the end.'

'In July. Her husband gone almost at once,
and no money found behind him in the house.'

'And a stone put up to mark the ground
where Lizzie had sat in the womb or nutshell,
like the kernel or waiting child.'

'Then the stone was moved to a more convenient spot,
and the plough no longer took account
of Bet Woodcock's particular place in that field.'

...these words for a wall, a dam
where the waters build but do not overflow,
for lock gates shut on the well of detail;

but the fullness of time is a wave that must come in.
These words for a net instead, fine-meshed as muslin,
to fish up the dead turn of head, the swallowed voice.

I felt the pattern and play of bones
under the still-fine fur: the point on his skull
between the ears, the jerky steep steps of his spine,
the neat rectangular box of pelvis,
peak of breastbone and so on;
muscles gone thin as silk – only furred skin
to hold the skeleton, to shape the cat.

The eyes dreamed wide and did not see the cushion
or my hand but something through and past them,
whatever it was as still as a pool in peat.
I was moved by his gaze, its range and bigness.
And the audible breath, and the visible jumping heart.

When the needle came to touch and meet that heart
his cry was outraged, and those eyes
caught an unseen object flung fast towards them.
Then the fur lay still and flat on a bag of bones.

This net fishes the shed claw from the floor,
the ball of greyed hair from underneath the sofa,
his seated shadow caught in the window's rectangle...

Shape-shifting

You see the same face across the generations –
her there, half a shadow and half concrete
in a real coat with mud-flecked facings,
a fraying hem, and lugging a leather suitcase
tied with string. She sings the same thread song

that her mother whispered above her cradle
in the winter dark about a thousand years ago;
the look in her eyes dissolves into a landscape
puddled with mud, far trees against the sky
and a rider going between them – herself maybe.

For she rises up wherever you might be watching
in a different costume, with various coloured hair
or lion's pelt, bird feathers – your glance catches
her even in the fireside cat that licks its paws
then turns its flexing gaze towards your face

before stalking out to the dusk and its dissolving.
And she is there at the gate, unlatching it and entering,
leaving her horse by the fence, feeling the cat's fur cold
against her legs as she advances up the shadowed path
to temporary safety. A woman within a home

for the briefest moment, she boils a kettle at the fire,
hangs her frayed coat on a peg and hunkers down
before the hearth to sing for anything arriving
out of the old winter dark – the gold-leaf lion
hauling a leather suitcase, a peacock trailing string.

Interrogation

Who lights a votive candle to the Rabbi Loew
that made the Golem out of clay and spittle?
Who puts a pebble on his tombstone's ledges,
reddish and lion-crowned, or leaves a pencilled
message on its strip of paper under such scraps of stone?

His grave is like a wayside shrine. The small flames
shake in the cemetery wind, the shreds of paper rattle.
The path that passes it turns to a trampled bog,
after the days of thunder rain, at just this spot.
What do they want of him who gave the Golem animation?

At night, when the gate in the wall is barred
and the candles have burned down to nothing
but a smear of grease on marble, who draws near
to read the flimsy pages anchored by little rocks?
The creature or the man or no one in a gaberdine.

I hesitate to describe again the cliché of the moon
walking the graveyard mounds, the march of shadow
clotting and unclotting in the veins through ranks of tombs.
But who would not prefer this to the mudman moving,
leaving his trail of clay unchanging on the ground?

Is this what they wish to avert by the eyes of flame
in daylight – the accretion of dirt that shambles
straight to them through the streets of Prague,
unstoppable unless its maker speaks the undoing words,
turning the earthen android into stuff of gardens?

The summer plots outside are thick with roses.
Their dense scents hug the soil then lift
with the little thermals to surmount the wall.
It is appropriate. Death's angel could only come to him
in the guise of that flower from his grand-daughter's fingers.

So I think the narrow papers interrogate the Rabbi
largely on horticultural affairs. How long
will this unbaked clay, though modelled,
hang together? Does a rose's perfection contain
the seeds of its own end? Tell us again.

Clothing

There should be, I assume, some correlation
between each object and the desire it calls
to itself, like moon dragging tides along behind;
but perhaps, they say, you are not so very weighty,
I've clothed you in layers like an onion's coats,
desire on desire, distorting your living centre
where the green shoot waits its moment, nearly stifled.

I don't know. Nightly dreams increase the freight,
complexity, compile a past we do not really share
in every kind of setting, every age; the huge weight
of them pulls on the neck and shoulders, hunching
both of us; we are attired for several Arctic winters.
Yet at the grain of the snowball, somewhere,
there is essential you, the person where I started.

Smaller perhaps, compacted, distillation of the colours
I have spread to make you from, taking less space
in passages and hallways, surrounded by less air
and echo everywhere, quieter; crowds do not part
inevitably letting you through nor do admirers gather
for your arrival... except me, equipped for snowman-
building with half at least a cloakroom's worth of coats.

Serial

1. *There was a man of double deed*
   Sowed his garden full of seed

He has made rows with string between two pegs
and sows along them carefully; but his wayward shadow
swings out from him at right-angles, shrinks then rears
as he crouches to let the seed slide through his fingers
into the little trench, then stands to ease his back
and take the next step in the garden. The lurch of shade
onto them disturbs the black ants carrying a moth away,
and they leave it, wind at ground level shivering its wings
to seeming life. Some of the seeds are skittering out of line,
the string disregarded – carrots may come up among the onions.

When gardening Eben Wilmet wears a business suit –
charcoal grey with a chalk stripe – and a tie
that's vaguely regimental or old-school. This is not
his incarnation on the street when he posts the letters
in Letraset capitals and cut-out newspaper words
such as 'prostitute' and 'child-molester', 'homosexual'.
He changes his costumes the better to watch himself behave –
either playing the role to the hilt in dirty raincoat
and dark glasses, or standing out against it, in the garden.

'Double, double, toil and trouble.' When carrots come up
among the onions, the girl too will have arrived
to visit the potting shed that's almost concealed
in its caul of convolvulus vines with shivering wings
of ephemeral sheet-white blooms. 'I have a lap of seed
and this is a fair country.' Eben watches himself and the girl
make pale star patterns in the shed's earthy gloom,
his hands on her skin the same as when his fingers
crush a convolvulus trumpet, coming out of the open door
to meet his shadow lying on the ground, to the left then to the right.

2. *When the seed began to grow*
'Twas like a garden full of snow

Daphne Christopher remembers her Wendy right from the first
realisation in the new weight of her breasts, the sense
of extra liquid stored all over between bone and skin,
the flutter below her waistband before the urgent kicks
when the shape of a baby's footsole could be traced
against her palm, when she would watch her belly
lurch to the right then to the left, the waistband laid aside.
And Tom remembers some of this – at least the beating
of that belly against his backbone in the night, the heat
of a third circulation system in the bed between them.

I planted a mango stone in a pot of bulb fibre
after the hyacinths were over. Once started it grew
seven inches within seven days, a not-quite-realistic pink
like rhubarb without the ridges. I was nearly afraid
to go away for Easter and leave it to its rampaging.
Later it became pot-bound and died. The flowers for funerals
are white lilies, white carnations; white orange-blossom
is for brides, and daisies are what she used when needing
to make predicitons – 'He loves me. He loves me not.'

I am avoiding mentioning the mourning, that winter
inside them, a closed garden heaped with snow
and printed all over with the futile fan-tracks of birds,
the paw-pocks of stalking cats. They contain it,
as the white hospital encloses the growing cancer,
unable to dig out from underneath the drifts
the unknown thing that's there. Their snow is salt
and, sown in the earth, renders the garden barren
where Wendy Christopher blithely arrived for summer
in those remembered days before she was quite lost to them.

3. *When the snow began to melt*
   'Twas like a ship without a belt

He had treated it like a building, supposed it was a house
when he went down its passages, carrying a covered tray
to the captain who liked his breakfast in bed on Sundays.
He had no doubt that there was ground beneath him
when he laced his leather shoes, nor worried
that his watch would stop if once immersed in ocean.
There were levels after all, and stairs, and a band played
for waltzing couples in the ballroom; the lights came on
when you flicked a switch and taps gushed fresh water.
Then it fell apart and turned to salt liquid overnight.

Tom Christopher had been one of only twelve survivors
from the crew of the cruise ship, *Caribbean*, wrecked
in a freak storm on an otherwise windless night.
It is long ago now, but he easily remembers
how the cold climbed up his legs hand over hand
and sharp stars leaned nearer, leering at him on his back,
the life-jacket buoying his shoulders and little waves
lipping against his chin, again, again. He thinks often
of it now, with Wendy gone, the shock somehow the same –
what was solid struck, jumbled and upturned, then drowned.

Even their snowy garden has not kept its frozen dignity:
the white grown smutty shrinks in random patches
to reveal irrational scraps of paving or dormant sticks
of weeds. When it melts and Daphne finds that she is crying,
it's for an odd spotted Wendy sock behind the laundry basket
or a girl on the bus and not at all like her, but running
a hand through her hair in the selfsame way. No order
or proportion or sense of hierarchy. Why should the snow
linger there on that lump of turf when the gutters are running?

4. *When the ship began to sail*
   'Twas like a bird without a tail

In Danish church after Danish church Jonas Hinds comes upon
the intricate votive ships that hang where the aisles cross
before steps rise towards the altar. He likes them but
they also nudge at him in ways less pleasurable.
As a boy he would sail his boats with particular intentness –
the matchbox with a curve of paper sail spiked by a stick,
on the puddle that always formed outside his house
in heavy rain, for one example; later the replica battleship
that an uncle had brought him after service overseas.
But he stopped on that one day entirely and forever.

'How many strawberries grow on the salt sea?
How many ships sail in the corn?' His had sailed
in the dry street, at least. Lacking a running gutter,
he had held the fragile boat a little out from the kerbstone
and talked it through the imaginary locks and under bridges.
Then the other boys had gathered and shown him
the caught pigeon, told their scheme of plucking
its tailfeathers out, to see if it could afterwards stay upright
or would fall forward on its beak again and again
like the wooden pecking-bird on the garden weathervane.

He remembers his cousin Eben's avid face across the pavement;
otherwise, only the bird's protesting open beak, the throb
of its throat, its feet beating the air as they began.
Then the big hands coming down to his immense relief
and snatching the pigeon away. There were four grey feathers
on the ground. Their shoes were scattering in all directions.
Joe's father snapped his boat in half for punishment,
solemnly, and he was glad of it, setting ships aside.
He started instead to watch for birds in hedges, on the ridge tiles.

5. *When the bird began to fly*
   'Twas like an eagle in the sky

The boy Jonas Hinds became an adult falconer,
and in the summer he gives displays, with a pouch
of dead mice on his hip and leather gauntlet to his elbow,
looking something akin to his birds himself – fierce eyes,
high-bridged nose, the trick of a watching stillness
stopped in full life for a moment on the top of a hill
or a high branch. He is taciturn except to his creatures,
who with heads cocked listen to his language of clicks
and whistles, of bubbled syllables, harsh signal cries.

I see him as a sort of icon, away from the crowds
in one of those open places you come over a crest to find
and think 'There should have been a battle here' –
slopes the right gradient for a charge and the plain
at the bottom wide enough for carnage. He strides
away from me and all the rest into such spaces,
then the great birds come to his wrist for their assignments:
the hawk, the merlin, owl and, of course, the eagle –
hugest of all, watching back over Joe's dark head
and assessing its flight to the sun or plunge to the sea.

There's not much money in it, unless hired by Arab sheiks
to join their hunting, so his room in the barn,
where the birds are dim stirring ghosts on their pole perches,
is a matter of bed, chair and table, some books and little else.
The barn wall is dense with ivy's secondary growth,
and nobody sees who comes there to him in the dark
or hears any human conversation. When he goes from home
a thin stranger youth attends to the mew then disappears
again on his return. He watches the hooded shapes lean in unison
towards him. 'Lully, lullay, the fawcon hath born my mak away.'

6. *When the sky began to roar*
'Twas like a lion at the door

'He bar him up, he bar him down' as this great wind does
with everything – a plastic carrier bag snatched from someone
and raced past the eighth-floor windows, slates peeled
from the church roof and hurled as discuses across the street.
Within the barn the hawks on their perches huddle thinner
as the air turns fast about the spindles of their bodies.
Jonas puts up shutters to bar the draught and makes a dark
as intimate as velvet against the eyeballs – but still
the knuckles and the shoulders and the feet of the wind beat the
boards.

Eben's garden is shredded, shed leaves drifting the paths
and verticals leaned on until they cant then flatten.
The big tree whips its branches like Medusa's head of snakes,
and the potting shed throbs like the box waiting for Pandora
to loose its contents on the world in a whirlwind rush.
In his room the corners of letters are lifted and fall back,
a pen rolls on the table, the newspapers shift in their piles:
his door is stout and double-locked – only a blade
of air slides underneath it and along the hinge edge,
only a single lion claw slits the membraned closure.

Seeing that it's no wolf at the door, Tom and Daphne
open up to the great beast padding through their house
in all its tawny gold and courage. Its sun-browned sprawl
in their garden might melt the snow at last
and make them lift their heads above the enclosing hills.
It has Wendy-coloured hair and a roar that takes up
all their breath in its defiance. On the day of the big wind
Tom Christopher finds his rage and starts to write,
on large sheets battened down with cups and milk bottles,
the letters to everyone about the search for his lost daughter.

7. *When the door began to crack*
   'Twas like a stick across my back

It seemed an important dream: wounded, he came to me
for help and safety; I kept him in the innermost room
and barred the series of doors that led to him, but later
I could not find the way back myself, the locks too many.
I sit up in bed in the dark and think about it:
door barrier or door opening, and how to keep the balance
between its dual uses in a life growing too private, too enclosed –
a nunnery walks about the littered streets in full daylight
on a weekday, not once creaking wide its disguising grille
or guiding a route through complicated cloisters to my cell.

And the wounded hero? Ah, here's where I've made the rod
for my own back. Come clean. I love the falconer
who gave up even shipping's sociability as a boy.
He has the locks and shutters to match mine,
the drawbridges, portcullises, iron bolts and chains,
the dark barn with its moat of field surrounding.
I sit up in bed in the night and consider strategy:
when I break through the barriers that have held me
just obsessed, watching him from afar, I'll have to tell him.

When in the morning the letter comes through the door –
'You were Wendy's friend. Please think back to what she was doing,
to where she used to go, who and what she talked about' –
I lay it aside for the moment, completely immersed
in my larger project, of laying siege to Joe's defences
in some believably natural manner, not courting humiliation
or telling lies. It's easy to feel no more than fifteen or so,
ritually inscribing 'I love him' in a diary last thing at night,
writing 'Jonas Hinds' on the inside covers of all my school
exercise books, or carving it on a branch – that stick again.

44

8. *When my back began to smart*
   'Twas like a penknife in my heart

Hands and face hotter than the weather justifies,
I walk over the endless openness of the field
to Jonas's barn in its disguise of ivy. I've found no pretext
for my presence there, but have come anyway,
the dream a goad behind me. Now or never, says my head,
take up your bravery at once and use, or lose, it.
It's not, after all, as though he's an absolute stranger;
there are things we can talk about – old times, new countries.
But the shock-headed youth who comes to the door
is someone I don't know, and I am speechless.

I am leaving a note – 'I must speak to you about something.'
He is rolling up wadded newspaper laid under perches
to absorb the droppings, replacing it with fresh sheets.
Friendly enough, he, one at a time, unhoods the hawks for me.
I move in to stare into their unrelenting agate eyes
out of another morality entirely. 'Don't touch them,' he says –
the tip of each beak is a needle, each separate talon
has a stranglehold upon its pole. A worm of fear
of Jonas enters me. When we drink tea quite silently
together, the birds behind us shift and lightly murmur.

There was that battleground that Joe walked into
in my vision. I think of it, of the otherness of his creatures,
retracing my journey with my courage leashed –
though not the loving. And find a pretext waiting.
The letter says, in Letraset capitals and newspaper cut-outs,
'If you're looking for Wendy Christopher, ask Jonas Hinds.'
As much a weapon as a claw, a knife, a beak, a needle,
it makes little slashes in herringbone pattern on my heart,
so sharp it's shock I feel, a stop of breath before the bleeding.

9. *When my heart began to bleed*
'Twas death and death and death indeed

A falcon, its jesses trailing, swoops in circles over us
before it settles on the barn's ridgepole. The ivy's thickness
makes a shade wide enough to sit in. Jonas holds the paper
with its anonymous lettering in both hands. Lines
from the sides of his hawk nose draw his mouth down
at the corners. He looks at the message again,
then as before he looks through the message to the ground
that's arid and dusty under the ivy with only a woodlouse
going about its grey business into the deeper shadow.

He talked about the pain it gave him to see her name
written, having tried to omit her memory from his life
but failed completely. He had grown used to her fleeting
ghost in the barn – the flag of bright hair always caught
for a moment in the sunlight before she went out
of his door into the day. She was ever going away.
At first he had pursued her presence, then he learnt
she stayed seconds longer if he could just sit quiet
and receive the tawny gold and energy that was Wendy,
passing through his life again and not gone, thank God.

Though she had left him – 'nothing more about me to find out'
he said. Two months before her disappearance
she had said goodbye and really stood for the last time
in his doorway, before following her curiosity elsewhere.
'But it didn't stop me loving her. I'll always do that.'
The bleeding starts from that arsenal of one weapon.
I sit beside him and begin to leak my heart away
on his dry ground – though going inside the nunnery
of my head to properly spurt and puddle and lie down,
drawing the grille tight shut behind me with a final clang.

The Glass Children

1

The persistence of the glass children
pressing their rigid fingers
against the resilience
of the woman's body.

They leave their cicatrice on her skin,
the star-print scar
that's whiter than
the flesh around it

and dead to the touch
to the scratch of a live fingernail
– not glass but horny substance,
not glass, not glass at all.

That rings and squeals
for a sliding wet finger
against the slippery limbs
of the fragile children

bathed in a basin
with the daily dishes,
bobbing up amid the soapsuds
over and over and over.

2

Queen Anne sits up
in her sumptuous bed
recovering again
from stillbirth.

The little robes
are laid away,
the cradle shoved once more
behind a curtain.

In the window
the grey agitation of the air
is snow fine as smoke
against the glass.

Somewhere beyond the room
a child is crying,
but the waiting-women
preserve a grave indifference

in their faces
as they bend to her and minister;
it is not a real child,
they seem to say,

there was never a child at all
in this particular palace,
whipped grey-white with snow
and skinned over by the ice.

3

Sublimation is making
glass figures that disappear
against the air,

that can be shelved,
along with their inhabiting spaces,
higher than eye level...

until the dust begins to define them,
lying along their limbs
and ringing the little mouths

and sifting downward,
calling the attention up
to the top shelf with the glass children.

So there they are,
the meant-to-disappear-against-the-air:
they are grimacing, they're beckoning;

their heads of young hair powdered old
lean out as gargoyles do
from the sheer drops of cathedrals.

They cannot be ignored any longer
in those ghostly dustcoats that they wear
like small removal men.

The Silent Woman

1

It accrues, the silence,
as *papier-mâché* does – postage-stamp-sized square
upon postage-stamp-sized square, and again,
again, into a gummy carapace, drying.

Once it was only one layer thick,
almost transparent; once, before, it was not there at all
– the very air was garrulous and her lips kissed that,
breathing, speech, embraces barely differentiated.

But she can hardly remember then:
memory too must push through silence and may be
discouraged in the dense maze of gum, the thorn thicket
keeping familiar princes back and away from kissing.

2

The child shielded the doll's head with one hand from the rain,
though the hood of her own mackintosh was still flat
upon her shoulder-blades. They had stepped
from the greengrocer's doorway into a downpour like
glass curtain behind glass curtain over and over.

'Oh,' she cried, and 'oh' again, while her sister danced
with covered hair under the falling water.
'It's Christmas and weddings and silver paper suddenly,
but I think my doll will melt in all this wetness.'
Her mother said, 'Don't talk nonsense!' and the littler girl
turned round and round with her feet in dazzling puddles.
The child in question started to apply the paper silence.

3

'We slung a curtain on a string across the room
to achieve some privacy for each of us.
I would sit sealed-off and try to hear her reading,
to listen to her sewing with silent thread and needle.

'Her quiet tantalised – though surely not on purpose –
until the whole of my existence in that place
was waiting for a movement's rustle, watching
the dark for light strained through hung fabric.

'I grew to want her for the shadow that she made
upon my mind, the faintest she-suggesting staining
of the air in front of me, wherever I might look;
my marriage, in the end, was to such ghostliness.'

4

In fact she spoke a good deal within the sounding-box
of her skull; she recognised her own real accents
in the soft contralto retailing judgements while
the face she assumed hung expressionless over the table
like the Baptist's head offered on a platter to them all...
and he kissed it as Salome nuzzled those cooling lips,
thinking something had been attained by decapitation.

Inside, her voice buried deeper as the worm
or mole does, leaving a smaller and smaller echo
to surface for a cast of earth at the back
of her eyes. She doubted any change was noticed
in the glazed gaze on the dish pushed to one side.

5

The doll her daughters played with – putting it to bed
in the pram, taking it out to have its clothes changed,
showing it the garden, and so on – had grown
near faceless with this use, eyebrow and mouth paint gone.

She hated it, without reasons she could speak –
little homunculus, grey-pink foetus – pulled the quilt
up and up to cover its forehead, obtrusive in the nursery cot,
her look drawn there despite the other tumbling toys around.

And when they paraded it in a new dress for her,
she could not praise, but turned away to book or needle,
erecting a thorn thicket of interlacing branches,
a curtain to withhold and hide even her children.

51

6

What gets left behind is often not intended to be found;
despite the old wives' saws, clean underwear is not donned
for every fresh foray into the streets of traffic.
The moment itself selects the meal in preparation,
what half-written letter is there lying on the desk.

In her case it was the doll-sized babies' bones,
wrapped-up in layers of paper and stowed in a chest,
that remained after she withdrew her quiet into
the absolute silence. It rained again that day,
and they could not understand what they had found.
Without her heard interpretation, everything was conjecture,
all metaphors of gum and princes, melting, a severed head.

Pen and Paper

Before the ladder to the platform closed in by fleering voices,
the tying of the feet, the laying on the tilted board face down
but with no place for cheek or lip to rest on,
before the oblique blade, the bloody basket;
arrived at the foot of the scaffold, Madame Roland asked
that she might have pen and paper to record
'the strange thoughts rising in her'.
                              Request refused,
as if it were some clever-dick trick of postponement;
the page remaining at the stationers, the quill untrimmed,
the strange thoughts in the skull as in a vase
that spilt them quite illegibly under the guillotine
a moment later.
                    A fate she knew could not be much delayed,
she would not read her own words back to her
at leisure after, what she felt urged to keep
could not be kept by her more than a minute's space;
but nonetheless she wanted pen and paper, meant
to snatch out of the blood-stained air those phrases
that would cage the strangeness lifting through her now.

For only words could net and hold the foreign birds
long enough in her sight for naming, recognition
under the single lightning-flash that time had left her;
only with pen and paper could she possess her death,
the momentary owner of a basket loud with wings
that the imminent blow would knock from her hands and scatter.

'They Say the Owl was a Baker's Daughter'

*'And thorns shall come up in her palaces, nettles and brambles
in the fortresses thereof; and it shall be an habitation of dragons,
and a court for owls.'* ISAIAH, 34.13

1

An empty bakehouse like a weekday church,
as chill to the touch as a milkchurn,
with the same bluish shadows as skimmed milk,
an echo as of a tin cup tapped by a spoon;

yet furred throughout with flour, blurred
as a breathed-on mirror, a steamed-up window:

the setting for the owl –
itself a slowed white flicker,
some shadow's reversed image
on a spiral of unexposed film.

It is night. The light
has drained into metal vessels:
lean over that great mixer
to catch its dying gleam –
some fallen star going
widdershins down the black plughole.

The owl wakes in its ruin,
the broken bakehouse wall,
where the window that was
peeled back, fraying bricks,
its whitewash dropped dunes of new flour;
the whole of the dark flooded in.

There are black loaves baking
in the ovens' doorless caves.
The owl attends them, busy
between this slab and space,
its white flight-feathers quivering
like the shapes in antique movies
recovered just in time, their silver edges eaten.

2

When I was ten or so
my best friend was a baker's daughter;
she nibbled raw pastry for pleasure.
We played in the vacant bakehouse in the afternoons,
riding down chutes meant for loaves, or rolling
in the loft's fat waves of flour-bloomed sacks.

She wanted to be a ballet-dancer –
might have been,
but for the off-white filaments of dough
that bound her, hand and foot,
to the little shop with their home stuck to it
and the big, low bakehouse,
like a grounded ship behind.

The abattoir-keeper's daughter made a third –
with no similar skein of flesh to hold her.
She was the first vegetarian I knew;
though her skin shrunk back white on her bones
when she told us, how market-gardeners and farmers
fed their land with the slaughter-house blood.
She disliked owls, for their killing,
the carrion smell of their nests.

And I was a grocer's child, a grocer's grand-daughter.
Our shop was across the road from the start
of a wood, where the jays laughed by day
and owls screeched and hollered throughout the night.
It was down the hill to the bakehouse
with pavements, roads and dwellings all around;
there the birds' dawn chorus was thin at best...
In the end that daughter had to go to bakers' college.

3

Walls beyond walls all around;
and men and women, children
strategically placed, observing
or turned away from the owl
in a cage in the pet department.

Mongooses flicker like flames
around a plate of fruit in their place
to the right. The owl is a stone
beside them, past breathing,
beyond the memory of prey,
any hunt for such as these.

I watch the agate eyes.
I stand foursquare before the cage
to stare back into them. No one
is there...But a tunnel is drilled
through my chest; the clothes
shrink back, the flesh, the bars
of ribs unlock to the owl's looking.

I believe I feel a rush of air
just underneath the heart...
then the slight brush of feathers.
In the cage, no one is there.

4

She carried the owl in her head –
gone one better than Athena,
with the occupied shoulder –
felt the pressure of its flat face
in the space between her eyes.

It was having two skulls
and all that that entailed;
there was ever the addition
to herself to bear in mind: that owl
at her brain through the night.

Though she went on regardless –
and almost unregarded – a black-eyed,
pale-fleshed figure among the loaves,
bending modestly to her works
of bread and pastry: the baker's girl.

The baker's girl, her father's daughter –
always defined that way,
despite the inner owl, its eyes

looking out through hers, its talons
closed tight on her thinking...

Only the day brought relief:
when the sleeping owl was simply
weight, the head's extra heaviness
upon her neck – an overblown
big flower wearying its stem.

And she came from the bakehouse's
nightwork into the light,
closing down within and stilling,
as houses and roads awoke
around her, the world shook its feathers.

5

The barn owl against the snow
is white no longer. November gone,
it has fallen silent, and hunts in daylight
for the scarce vole, the rat, the rabbit...
Where are they?

                  No more do small birds
mob it by day, asleep in the densest tree.
Like a shuttle among the bare branches,
it searches the scarcely-featured ground
for necessary prey.

               In its roosting place:
the mound-mattress of old pellets
falling apart to fur and bones – and
nothing more, no freshness, and no
blood upon the stones.

                 See the spaces
of it: those immense secret ears,
its gape like a snake's, and all
the cut-out shapes of air about its body –
rectangle and triangle and square.

6

And if it should let go, take off,
stretch its wings to their width
and lift through her suddenly
transparent skull to quarter
the bakehouse's light-barred floor...?

She had felt the bird shift unquietly
as she leaned over dough set to rise.
A pulling-apart was beginning,
the hard separation, resisted –
like her halving of that bread-mixture –
by strands and strands and strands,
off-white filaments that clung and
thinned, and broke apart at last.

The top of her head seemed temporary
as a cap, as cold as a shaven tonsure.
Her skull was the crystal Aztec version
she had seen once in a magazine –
delicate, fragile, and about to shatter
as the bones of the owl flew through it
and away.

7

Rumours of a white owl in the district
are shown to be true – and, at the same time,
turn to lies – when the broken body
is lifted from the road, after the lorry,
whose wide lights dazzled it, has gone.

Its broad wing span is stretched
between the fingers. The pale plush heart
of its face falls back on its snapped neck
in the dark. The eyes are dull coals.
Ferocious talons hang there, hang there.

An absence has its weight in the hands.
A presence is no more than an idea, unease
for the two or three in the midnight lay-by.
Yet the bird's body in their midst is less white,
less substantial, than what flickers in the film
running a touch too fast at the corner of the eye.

On the Border

The revolver, the just-emptied casket of woman's ashes,
the beach at dusk under a squally wind;
the bathroom, a slew of toothpaste-streaked water,
a motorbike starting up at the back of the house:
the first, the distant, overlays the second which is near,
at hand, the tooth-glass insensibly in the fingers;

and the ashes can reassemble, climb up each other's ladder
into bone and flesh and hair, the woman stride
the slope of the dunes from the sea's thump and spillage

if I desire it, stilled momentarily at the white basin
by my open-eyed dream of strewn objects in the sand
and of the man whose hand is on the cold revolver
in November, the pulse that follows the motorbike's kick-start.

He does not grow old in my possession, this man of air
who nonetheless on the beach can upturn the open casket
to show her ashes quite gone away in the squall,
blown to less than himself who is nothing

but stronger than this house, falling apart as if card-built
so his wind can reach my mouth over the roofs of the town
and all the rest that is only real landscape
trying to hold out against the imagined, the dream

minutely articulated, organised fiercely, revised
and polished till it shines out diamond-hard
to write on the glass of my windows and mirrors,
on the tumbler whitened by toothpaste in my hand
(that even now, in the sand, is gathering up the woman).

Salome

At the last she was a pillar of salt
– that white, that still after the whirling
and the silk shed from her
with a petal's first curling back then falling
fast, down directly to the ground
to lie rucked and shrunken with soiled edges;

a sort of Lot's wife of the mind,
since that was where their thinking held her:
with nudity accomplished
at the eye of a storm of subsiding veils,
the rose that ticked unwound to leave intact
its bare stripped core for the eyes' examination.

The Hairy Woman at Court

JOHN EVELYN, 15th September 1657: '*I saw the hairy woman, 20 years old, whom I had before seen when a child. She was borne at Augsburg in Germany. Her very eye-browes were comb'd upwards, and all her forehead as thick and even as growes on any woman's head, neatly dress'd; a very long lock of haire out of each eare; she had also a most prolix beard, and mustachios, with long locks growing on the middle of her nose, like an Iceland dog exactly, the colour of a bright browne, fine as well-dress'd flax. She was now married, and told me she had one child that was not hairy, nor were any of her parents or relations. She was very well shap'd, and plaied well on the harpsichord, &c.*'

Do you remember King Solomon's way of disproving
or proving the Queen of Sheba's animal-pelted legs:
the mirror floor? She recalls it now and draws her skirts in
at the edge of the glassy ballroom.   A broad expanse
to cross and cover before reaching this king and his court
on the other side. She begins her glide of minute steps
towards them in their stillness, in their unanimous intensity
of gaze.   Listen to the hiss of hair and travelling silk
on the polished surface. She hears them imagining,
as Solomon's flunkeys did, the hidden forms of neither
beast nor woman, the petticoated mossy pegs
above her ticking heels.   She feels her freakishness
in full before them. It is the passport that brought her
to the palace, yet also a divisor far wider than
this endless floor like a midwinter frozen lake
she can nonetheless ford on her feet – as she does now.

Fingers

Beneath the theatre, the tank of seawater that awaits
its filtering into swimming-baths stuff, glaucous green
over the pale glazed tiles. They say it has conger eels
turned moon-white in the dark and grown far past
the escaping size, they say it is inhabited by blind fishes.

I saw a conger eel once, caught on a fisherman's hook.
It was like a gigantic nail, knotting itself and
knotting itself and flailing, muscled grey, out of water.
Even long dead and lying doggo in the bottom of a boat,
one can take off a man's fingers in a final reflex bite.

I feared even its proximity in the air over that bare inch
or so of beach – as it seemed to me in my felt exposure.
I was weak water and it was iron alive, swinging
wilder and wilder on the line, knotting, unknotting.
I prayed for it to get away, and it did, slipping the hook.

It came from the bottom, from underneath the surface,
like the B-movie beasts from two-thousand fathoms
or the Kraken awoken from its slow and biblical sleep
into lifting from darkness to the filtered, trembling light
where undersides of boats hang as rain clouds in a sky.

There's an old flat-bottomed wooden skiff afloat
on the theatre cistern. Abandoned, for who would
skull about in an absolute salt-sharpened dark
where blind fish nudge the oars and etiolated eels await
the fingers dipping down from black air into black water.

Weight
(after a painting by Samuel Bak)

I shall look at paving stones differently,
having seen your ghetto painting, Samuel.
I shall think of their undersides, their pressure
on what lives below in the nearly darkness
of damp and must and something scuttling away.

Though they might be blond on top
in the level honey light of early morning,
they press nonethelesss on the heads underneath,
they bear down in *peine forte et dure*,
the long death plus bread and a little water.

I have no right to write or speak of this,
no authority save your picture and its weight
against my eyes in the white-lit gallery,
eclipsing other works. I walk about
with its blocks and inner black inside me.

For on the surface it is cream and terracotta,
and the fabric makings for the yellow star
are flung down on the stone there, casually;
the light is bright, although unnaturally even;
it's like a stone-built dolls' house, square and small.

But smaller still, as if far distant,
is the city found in the crack at the heart of the box:
its swarming windows black as flies on yellow
and the red streaks running down the walls
like blood; all verticals askew, unbalanced.

It becomes a mad hive, to be dismantled,
since its winter bees have died with no honey
in the comb, and lie – what few are left –
as husks on the hidden ground. Yet they've found
no one can lift the heavy nest of flagstones.

I walk about and walk about outside it,
the neat container, made to hold compressed thousands
in the walled-in dark. It is not small at all.
The gallery's floor is cracking, the earth below;
the weight it carries scars and fissures everything.

Sunday Morning

They feel my gaze upon them in their dark sarcophagi
of lead and such material, some stuck with velvet
and black fringes: most unquiet, most unserene
in vaults equipped for observation through grilled windows.

They loom and wait thus, like so many Draculas,
under the iron and marble. Smell of damp and must
sifts through the gratings from the subfusc underground
like their breath only just suppressed in the deception.

And the shadow from them rises to accompany me outside
and sieve the sunlight into motes of restless darkness.
Hard to shake them, hard to walk away from them unladen,
turning my face to water and the wheatfields tumbling down.

Until the archway and the swallow's delicate daubed nest,
the bird itself to and fro as closed dart and then barbed arrow
and then out over the lake to join its myriad fellows
weaving their luminous nets with high sharp cries.

They fish away the subterranean in my eyesight
and I recall: not far from here, before history or churches,
a little dead child whose name no one remembers
was laid to rest on a swan's white wing, for flight.

Denmark 1990